TWIN FLAME
Hell

TWIN FLAME
Hell

LIFE WITH A REPTILIAN ALIEN

ANGIE MAXFIELD

Twin Flame Hell: Life with a Reptilian Alien
Copyright © 2024 by Angie Maxfield

Contact information: https://angiemaxfield.com

Book Cover Design: German Creative

ISBN:
Hardcover: 9798326311757
Paperback: 9798324821296

First Edition: June 2024
10 9 8 7 6 5 4 3 2 1

For

Ellie

There is no point in writing a book
unless you must write that book
or go mad or perhaps die.

by: Robertson Davies

SIGN UP FOR MY AUTHOR
NEWSLETTER

Be the first to learn about Angie Maxfield's
new releases and receive exclusive content
like sneak previews.

www.angiemaxfield.com

Contents

INTRODUCTION
TO THE
INSANITY

WITHIN A COMMUNITY OF TWIN FLAMES
that encourages the acceptance of abuse to reach a
state of Divine Union, insanity can no longer hide in
the shadows. Having known many long-term
married couples, those couples started in a state of
stability and love. In contrast, I have not met
couples who started in a state of disharmony, such
as the Twin Flame stages of runner, chaser,

abandonment, cheating, and abuse, to then heal each other and move into harmony. To the core of logic, the Twin Flame Union concept is illogical.

This book contains my Twin Flame story spanning from 2009 until 2022. Having opened to my psychic abilities in my twenties, I have included magical or psychic stories as well as sections relating Twin Flames to narcissists and negative extra-terrestrial aliens. At the end of the print version of this book, there is a Twin Flame Journal.

Not attempting to sound overly dramatic, I am content to be alive after the soul-crushing verbal abuse, control, and threats of physical abuse from my Twin Flame. I sincerely believe negative Aliens control him, or he is part Alien himself. My only wish is to assist the readers in gaining the knowledge that aligns with your chosen path. Not the path that serves these dark forces.

TWIN FLAME
MAGICAL
MOMENTS

MANY TWIN FLAMES SPEAK OF UNEXPLAINED occurrences once they become aware of their Twin. Common are synchronicities, feeling the Twin's presence when not physically together, psychic abilities opening, or a new desire to follow a spiritual path. My psychic abilities began opening while I was attending college. After college, I went on to teach before becoming a hypnotist and energy worker. The following are magical, psychic moments I experienced after meeting Bobby while on the Twin Flame Journey. I feel these psychic moments pulled me deeper into the relationship deception, AKA the "Twin Flame Hell." Towards the end of this book, notice the chapter named: "Twin Flame Alien Interference: The Last Magical Moment" where I look at what I believe is the truth behind the Twin Flame Dynamic: Dark Aliens.

Twin Flame Plan to Come to Earth

Years after finding Twin Flames, I heard of the Twin Flame plan. Some Twin Flames had visions of their plan to be together on Earth. If others had visions of their plan, I wondered whether I could experience a vision of our plan to come to Earth and unite into the Divine Union.

I had never lit a candle expecting a magical moment at that time. Nor had I peered into a crystal ball. All of that seemed insane, but I do feel the power of fire. I lit a candle intending to see my plan to enter Earth with my Twin Flame, Bobby. In a flash, I was not on Earth anymore. Instead, I was in another realm with Bobby.

He looked like his Earth version except his eyes were at peace with a purity about his face. His tan-colored clothing looked casual with a loose-fitting flow in his long-sleeved shirt and pants. Bobby had his hands out waiting for me.

Then, I realized I was only a voyeur with Bobby to my right and my soul to my left deciding on a body for this Earth experience. Several faces flowed by quickly as if someone were flipping through a photo album at a speed so fast that the faces almost merged as one. A blue face stood out startling me as I discovered some of the faces were not human. At that moment, I remembered being on other planets, which brought wholeness as I realized I was more than this one life I was about to embark on.

Bobby patiently waited as he was ready for this incarnation before me. A slightly sheer white sheet hung from above as if hanging from an old clothesline. After choosing my body, I was behind the sheet pushing towards Bobby as the outline of my human form started to appear. The sheet became more sheer. Then, as the sheet changed to a transparent state, my human female body emerged. Like a ballet dancer, I gracefully glided to take his

•

hands in mine. Suddenly, I fell back to Earth with a hard thud, sitting on my floor with the candle.

Hologram Floating

After my Twin, Bobby, and I began dating, he left for an overseas military assignment. I was teaching at the time. One day, I was walking through the offices in between classes. I saw Bobby as a vision to my left side looking like what I would describe as a hologram. Turning towards me, Bobby was floating next to me as I walked. The vision was clear and solid, moving as I moved. Intensely, he looked at me while I only glanced towards him, as I walked through the office.

Being the typical busy day at school, I had items to complete before my planning time ended. Having had spiritual moments before, I was at ease with the vision of Bobby next to me while I rushed through my day.

With the real Bobby working overseas in Afghanistan, he would have been asleep then due to the time difference. I wondered whether he was astral traveling while dreaming causing him to peak in on me that day.

Little Fat Gnome

Different than the hologram, Bobby and I traveled out of this world. My Twin Flame and I were holding each other one morning lying on his bed. Relaxing and chatting, the conversation stopped as Bobby physically changed into a different being I can only describe as looking like a gnome. His face, still human in appearance, was quite fat, as was his body.

Our surroundings changed with us no longer being on his bed in the bedroom. Instead, we were lying in circular areas of above-ground tree roots. The roots created a bed for us. Just as the roots were entangled, our arms and legs wrapped around each other. Feeling cozy and safe for several minutes, other root pods spread out around us enclosing gnomes.

In an instant, I was back on Bobby's bed with his face and body back to his normal human state. Expecting him to ask me where I went, or where we went, Bobby looked at me as if nothing had happened. Several minutes in another reality, wherever I was, became timeless as I traveled back to Bobby's bed. Could I have stayed there for days, even years, experiencing the other reality without affecting our time on Earth?

•

Our Wedding

This parallels the hologram when working at a school. There was a period when my Twin and I did not talk for two years. The first year away from Bobby was devastating as if the entire universe, God, and anything else that could have hurt me, had taken a blunt dagger and chopped my heart into nothing but a pulp of blood. In the second year, I began dating, almost forgetting about him.

Sometime during that first year, when I still had feelings for him and faith that we would reunite, I went to the church we both belonged to. At that church, they have prayer groups. Walking to the front after the church service, I asked a prayer group to pray for my friend, calling Bobby my friend since we were no longer dating.

I asked for safety and assistance for whatever he was going through. Not listening to the prayer, I looked off to my left where I saw what seemed to be a hologram, an overlay of another timeline, or another realm. Being in a traditional long white dress, Bobby and I had just married.

The vision was clear and real as if I could walk up and touch the other versions of us although no one else seemed to see the vision. At that time, I assumed I was looking into the future. The vision seemed off though because when I thought of marrying him, I imagined we would be on a beach barefoot, in casual clothing...just myself and my Twin Flame.

Elephant Ganesha Beings

I've traveled and moved throughout my life. I grew up in Florida and have lived in Hawaii, Arizona, and Germany. I've traveled around Europe including snow skiing in the Alps and became sunburned on the beach in the Bahamas.

After visiting Arizona before moving there, this strange event happened when driving back home. I was dating Bobby, but he did not come on that trip. Once I arrived back home, he was angry I had not asked him to go when all he had to do was tell me that he would like to go. Although, I feel this experience would not have happened with him on the trip with me.

I usually plan my travels when driving so I'm not driving late at night. But sometimes there are interferences like traffic or fatigue. One evening, I arrived at a hotel a bit late. There were

•

only a couple of fast-food restaurants in that small
area that were open, plus a bar. After checking in at
my room, I drove to the bar looking for food and a
relaxing atmosphere. Besides an occasional drink, I
don't drink alcohol anymore.

I was a lush until the age of 21. Then I
noticed people, including a boyfriend, being stupid,
getting drunk, vomiting, and blacking out. That
along with a couple of my black-out drunken nights,
I cut down to one or two drinks. This information
regarding me not drinking anymore is stated to set
the stage that I was completely coherent the night
this story happened and during all the other magical
or psychic events in this book.

Sitting in the bar, I ordered street tacos and
silently watched people, as I normally do. There
was a low energy feeling in the bar. Although, I was
in a state of peace as I watched beings walking
through an open area. The beings were together in
groups of three or four per group with a total of
about 12. Not interacting with the humans, they
walked among us. No one else was aware of them.
They were not aware of me.

They looked similar to the Hindu God
Ganesha or similar to elephants with a nose hanging
down at least two feet long. Their bodies were tall
and slim standing a foot or more above the tallest

people in the bar. The colors of their bodies were purple, green, and a mixture of blue shades.

They did not seem to be causing a problem as I felt they had come in from another reality or another realm to feed off the low energy. The feeling of peace around me, I later learned, was a shield blocking them from seeing me as I watched. Each time these events happen where a door opens and I see two worlds, I have the peace shield around me.

Confirmation came a couple of years later when Bobby and I were in a shopping mall. We walked into a store that had T-shirts displayed on the wall. Shocked, I saw a T-shirt with a painted picture that looked almost identical to the beings that were in the bar. There were also symbols painted around the beings.

When I see visions, I have a level of disbelief. Then I resume back to my life here as a human. But seeing a shirt and knowing that someone else has seen the same beings, confirmed that night in the bar.

Bloody War Past Life

In the Twin Flame Community, some say this is your only lifetime with your Twin Flame, and some say we have many lives together. I know I've had other lifetimes with Bobby.

One day, I was sitting with a friend in my living room. We discussed how my Twin Flame would tend to choose money over his son and me by choosing contract work for the military overseas when he has the skills to work locally in the United States. He reasoned that in Afghanistan, he could make more money quicker. My reasoning was a loss of time with his nine-year-old son and me. Time, I considered priceless.

My living and dining area, where my friend and I chatted, is at least thirty feet long. While talking about money and war, an overlay or reality opened with a pool of blood spilling out in front of me as if someone turned on a faucet. The blood spawned at least six feet wide and the length of the thirty-foot room.

The path of blood led my eyes to the vision of a life with my Twin where he was a soldier. We were married with four children. One of our children is my daughter in this lifetime. His son from this lifetime was there. Those two children were about the same age. We also had twin babies that were under one year old.

Bobby told me he had to go off into another, yes another, war. I pled with him not to go. Starvation was rampant among the people in our village. The rain had not come when needed to water vegetable fields. Animals were dying off as well putting meat in short supply. Within our impoverished home, I saw old dirty clothes, empty cupboards, and empty eyes…empty of hope.

Bobby stayed working in the vegetable fields with us past when he needed to leave so we could collect the last of our crop before it went bad in the sun. Then he left one early morning before I woke.

During the time Bobby was gone, both of our babies died of malnutrition. Soon after, our daughter died. Her sadness of leaving that life as a child and her emptiness of being born to parents who did not provide vibrated through me at an intensity I could hardly stand. I broke out in tremors as tears ran down my face.

I was then left with one child, our son. Having lost track of time due to disorientation caused by starvation, it felt like Bobby had been gone for years. Our son tried to do odd jobs for people to bring in something for the two of us who were alive, but no one was thriving around our village to give him work or to give us food.

By the time Bobby returned, I was on my deathbed. Bobby visited the burial grounds of our three other children and then came in to tell me of the war. He said when he arrived to fight the war, his company of fellow soldiers were dead. I couldn't read on his face whether he was more upset our children were dead and I was dying, or was he more upset he arrived too late to help the soldiers. Possibly, it's neutral, and death is death.

As painful as it was, Bobby did his best to turn over bodies, to see who was dead so that he could give families closure by coming back with news of those who had died valiantly. My eyes followed what he said as I saw men missing limbs, surrounded by the stench of death, a smell like no other smell.

MY TWIN FLAME STORY

ALTHOUGH MY PSYCHIC ABILITIES came in years before, I did not meet my Twin Flame, until 2009. I call him Bobby for his privacy since this book is based on a true story of what I thought was love. The end regarding physical abuse is true as is everything here as I remember it with complete transparency.

To set up our background, we met at a non-denominational church. I was dating someone else for the first three years I knew Bobby. He and I would talk occasionally at the Sunday service or during church events. Later, I found it interesting that through the years we would randomly run into each other in a city of over three million people, sometimes at unusual places we would not regularly attend.

In 2009, I was standing at the back of the church having come in late. Bobby came in late and stood in the back next to me.

Leaning in close whispering Bobby said, "Have you married that guy you've been dating?" He surprised me with his question because I had forgotten I considered marrying the man I recently left.

I raised my hands and asked, "Do you see any rings on my fingers?" At that point, I felt a change in energy as if someone flipped on a light switch. I realized this gorgeous man had been here for three years while I dated a man I didn't want a future with.

"I have some movie coupons in my car if you want them for you and your daughter," he said.

My mind was still wandering through the possibilities of lost time—*we could have been together sooner*. I had flashbacks to a church event where we sat next to each other at dinner. Next to him, it was as if no one else was there.

That was almost three years earlier, the beginning of my relationship with the other man. That night, several of us met for drinks after dinner, including Bobby. I called my boyfriend pressuring him to meet us. I did not know it then, but something was holding Bobby away from me those three years earlier.

Focusing back on my fingers where I did not have a wedding band, I looked at Bobby wondering whether he felt something as well. "The tickets would be great."

I followed him out to his car thinking I would follow him anywhere. I tried to catch his blue-eyed gaze as often as I could. When we arrived at his old Ford sedan, he walked over to the passenger side and pulled tickets from the glove box.

As he handed the tickets to me, I said, "There's a kid-friendly event coming up here at church if you'd like me to email you some information," I couldn't let him leave without gaining his contact information.

As soon as I arrived home, I emailed him the information. The same evening, he emailed back and asked me to have pizza with him and his son.

I felt like a teenager and called my older sister. She told me it would be better to meet at my

•

house and have a pizza delivered so he and I could talk while our kids watch a movie or play a video game.

The night he came over the Twin Flame highs increased. We sat on my back porch while his son and my daughter, close in age, watched a movie. At that time, and soon after, I found similarities between us. We are the same age, days apart. Our fathers have red hair. We are both left-handed. Our fathers were our main loving and supporting force with us both having unstable mothers.

That night, Bobby confirmed he had thought of me over the years while I was still asleep to any connection. He looked intensely through me and said, "I wanted to ask you out several times, but I would see you at the church with that guy you were dating."

Something changed in my heart. Was my heart even there before? Was it just an organ going through the motions beating and moving, one man to another, with no real purpose…no real meaning? I breathed in love for the first time in my life.

He contacted me within the week asking me to dinner. That time would be without the kids. Dressing for the date differed from other dates because I considered more about what to wear.

Wearing a tight green shirt and jeans when I met him at the restaurant, he politely stared into my eyes instead of at my breasts. "I like how your hazel eyes change colors with what you wear. I thought they were golden, but they look green tonight," he said.

He noticed the little things. The things that count to women. I thought about our journey that I was sure would last forever into heaven on earth.

In a restaurant with the longest menu anyone could imagine, we ordered the same entrée and asked for an inch of room for cream in our coffee. More similarities.

"I have to tell you something just to clarify," he said. Here come the Twin Flame lows. "I don't want to start dating anyone right now."

My mind was racing through reasons why. "What's going on?" I was confused after the other night with him saying he wanted to ask me out in the past...him noticing my eyes...our attraction.

"I'm about to go overseas for six months. It's a military rotation."

I felt like I was falling...darker and darker where I was...barely a glimpse of light. Why was I here at dinner? Why was he at my house having pizza with our kids? He had started something and said things. Falling. Darkness.

•

Bobby was scheduled to leave in three months. Yet, he kept contacting me to get together. We became friends...close friends taking our kids out, meeting for coffee, or trying something new.

We lived near the Gulf of Mexico in Texas. On a day trip to the beach, he commented on us. "Your daughter just saw something between us."

"What are you talking about?" I asked. I was distracted looking at the menu inside a sandwich place we stopped at after the beach.

"She just gave us a look. She's watching us."

I let it go at that time. I still felt something for him, but he was leaving for six months. His occasional comments and seeing me every week were puzzling considering he said he didn't want to date.

Those three months went quickly with him leaving in a few days. He was supposed to leave for a one-month training out of state before going overseas. After that one-month training, Bobby thought he would be able to come back home for about a week before going overseas. We planned to hang out at my house without the kids before he left. I had a plan of my own.

I picked up food and beer before he arrived. After we ate and talked, I dropped the not-so-subtle request after he helped me to assemble a small desk.

We were standing in my upstairs study talking about my desk when I moved close to him with my body almost touching his. "I think you should kiss me before you leave."

He took a step back along with his hard rejection. "I'm not starting anything before I leave to go overseas."

Early on, he did say he didn't want to date because he was leaving. But I didn't understand why he was spending all this time with me to only be a friend. I could feel we were both attracted to each other.

Not physically able to speak, I walked down the stairs. Retrieving the remainder of the six-pack I had bought for him, I met him by the door as he was stepping off the last stair.

"Are you kicking me out?" he asked as I handed him the beer. I circled past him and started up the stairs to my bedroom as he let himself out the door.

•

RECONNECTING

PEOPLE THINK THEY CAN relate to rejection in relationships, but there's an intensity in the Twin Flame relationship I had not felt in the past. Although I didn't know what Twin Flames were then, I felt a unique energy move through me. I longed to be with him. Through my years of marriage and having lived with two other men, nothing compared to the level of love and pain that resided within the energy of Bobby and I coming together. His rejection caused an ache…a total emptiness that began to take over my life.

Bobby had said he may come back after his

thirty-day training before going overseas. After a few weeks, I watched the church audience closely looking for him in case he did return. I needed at least a friendship, I told myself. But my heart wanted everything from him.

Bobby showed up at the late church service four long weeks after he left my home. I waited until the end of the service to walk over. "I'd like to talk to you later today."

"I'll call you," he said with a chill in his voice.

I went home and waited. No call. I was a teacher at the time. During my lunch the next day, I called him. Before the call, I wrote a short note of what I would say if he answered his phone. Or if he didn't answer.

I nervously phoned him. No answer. In leaving a message I read verbatim from the note, "Hey. I'm sorry how things were when you left. I value our friendship and just wanted to chat with you while you're in town before you go overseas for six months." I choked back tears when I said: *Overseas for six months.*

Within the time it would take for Bobby to screen the call and listen to my message, he called back.

•

"How long are you in town?" I asked as calmly as possible.

"I leave Friday for Afghanistan."

In less than a week he would be gone from my life for six months...or forever. He could choose to not see me again. I could choose to cut him off as well because he would be gone for six months. With any other man, I would move on and not look back. "Do you want to meet for coffee and chat before you leave?" I asked.

"I can meet you at your house tonight if you want. We can figure out if we want to get coffee or a drink," Bobby said.

Some light came in. Being his friend, I could have a piece of my heart back. We decided to meet at <u>seven</u>.

He was late. I kept checking my phone afraid he would cancel.

Bobby rang the doorbell. My whole body shook afraid he would yell at me and end whatever we were because I pushed his boundaries about kissing.

The opposite happened. He came in the door and sat on my sofa. I sat at the other end half lying down with my feet near him. We chatted about his training while he was out of state.

"I wanted to call you while I was gone," he said casually as if our last day together was a missing date on the calendar. "I missed our talks."

"I missed talking to you also." I was feeling uneasy with his amnesia.

He moved to the middle seat on my sofa and reached his hand to my face. "Can we lay down here together?" he asked while he patted the sofa.

As soon as he asked, he was moving down next to me. I inched myself down the sofa so that we were facing each other.

Bobby held me for a while. Then he kissed me softly on my cheek. It was as if we were new swimmers moving carefully from the shallow end to the deep end. Then he kissed my lips. I had never longed so badly for a kiss, and now he was next to me. Time didn't exist. We kissed and caressed delicately running our hands over the PG parts of our bodies as if a snail's pace was the way to proceed.

I ended the night after looking at the time on my phone. "I have to get up at six for work, and it's after midnight."

"I want to see you again before I leave the country," he said as he stood.

"Only if you admit that you initiated that first kiss here tonight."

•

Letting out a small laugh he shook his head. "You attacked me...took advantage of my obvious virginity."

Then it was me joining in on the laughter. "I would love to see you again before you leave...of course," I said as I stood and kissed him.

"All I want to do is kiss you now. I see you differently," Bobby said as he took my hand, moving to the door.

Wednesday, he took me out to dinner, and we came back to my house for more light making out as if we were teenagers. Considering we just moved past the friendship stage, it didn't feel right to have sex with him leaving for six months even though I wanted him deep inside me.

Bobby asked me to come to the base Friday where he would be flying out. He told me he would leave my name on the family list at the gate. I liked the sound of being on a family list.

On Friday, my heartbreak was magnified after entering the room of sad faces. I had dated a military man years before, and I had been in the military myself causing me to be familiar with the fear and loneliness of leaving and being left.

Family and friends were in a room with huge windows that looked out onto the airfield. His son was there along with his dad and brother.

Hugging me before he walked out to the plane, he held me hard leaving me wondering if it was a forever goodbye. Bobby was going into a war in Afghanistan. Walking to my car after he left, tears poured out as feelings hit like lightning.

Bobby and I moved to a schedule of Skype videos and emails. At least we could see each other's faces on Skype.

A strange thing happened one evening. I had two friends over to watch a movie. When I left them to get us something from the kitchen, I felt the urge to check my email. Bobby had sent a message earlier I had not seen until that evening. His message read: "I wanted you to know I'm fine in case you see something on the news. Bombing happened on the base. It wasn't a big deal. I tried to let you know as soon as I had my turn to email the family. They are limiting our time online in these tech rooms so everyone can notify family as quickly as possible. We can probably still Skype tomorrow."

My fears when he left were coming true. I was confused though because earlier that day a robbery had occurred near where I lived. Police cars were blocking some of the streets when I was driving through my neighborhood to go for a run. As I parked my car at the neighborhood track, a helicopter that was flying away from me changed course and began flying toward me. A police car drove up near me, and two cops got out of their car.

They kept a distance from me as one asked if I lived on this block while the other talked on his walkie-talkie. I said that I have lived on 6th for a few years. He then told me to go home because there had been a robbery nearby, and someone had been shot. They must have confirmed I was not the threat they were looking for because the helicopter turned and flew the other way.

When I Skyped with Bobby the next day, I found out the timing of the bombing on the base occurred when I was at the track with the police while a criminal was in my neighborhood. The universe, or something, had these negative life events coordinated.

SIX MONTHS

Feeling like the longest six months of my life, love was building inside of my heart after our time Skyping and emailing. Just talking and writing to each other for six months without the traditional type of dating where people would go out together, caused me to feel we had learned more about each other in that short time. It felt as if we had known each other for years. The Aliens increase the familiarity between Twin Flames. Aliens abducted Bobby and me at the same time since we were children to not only create our connection but to create an emptiness where we would both feel like a part of us was missing when they separated us. Hence, the feeling of being a complete soul once we find our Twin.

Bobby had a solid date of when he would be home from Afghanistan. A military relations lady called me about his arrival since I was listed to pick him up at the civilian airport. She told me there was a plan for the families to be at the gate to meet the service members instead of us meeting at baggage claim.

All the civilians got off the plane first. Many civilians stayed to see us reuniting. A long line of camouflage flowed out of the gate reminding me of zebras hiding from predators. When our eyes met, I was no longer aware of anyone else.

We hugged while he pressed his cheek hard against mine. "This is surreal," Bobby whispered. "You're here."

Seeing each other almost daily, we returned to the normal things we enjoyed doing together— day trips to the beach or simple things like dinner or a bookstore. The innocent physical side was still intact mainly because he had found religion and no longer believed in sex before marriage. I believed in sex after marriage, before marriage, before dinner...anytime it felt right. But I considered following this different road since I had this unique connection with him. Bobby began talking about dates to get married like 8-8,11-11, or 12-12. I told him I liked the date of 11-11 since my dad would often notice the time when it is 11:11, and my mom would tell people that they live 11 miles outside of town.

Bobby was home for only a month when a change occurred in our relationship. His son's mom and son would be at a Boy Scout meeting, and we planned to meet them there. Bobby was obsessed with wanting his son to become an Eagle Scout. On the car ride over, I heard about the successful people who were Eagle Scouts including presidents. Once there, his son, Chuck, spent time with his mom and Bobby. I ran into a friend that I chatted with while Bobby was busy with his future Eagle Scout. The night was relaxing until he took me home.

Once inside my house, I offered him something to drink, and we sat down.

"Chuck's mom said she has a friend at work who wants to meet me and go out on a date," he said casually.

"Did you tell her you are dating me?" Looking at him, I couldn't read his thoughts besides seeing the surprise on his face. I thought to myself: *Did I wait six months for someone who I*

*feel love for...someone who is talking to me about
marriage dates...to have him go off with another
woman?*

His surprised face then changed to anger.
"I've been offered a contract job overseas that pays
big bucks. If I don't find a job here soon, I'm going
to take the offer."

"You just came home. I thought you were
home to stay." Rubbing my temples, a headache
was throbbing as I thought of him leaving...and
another woman.

"If I can't find a job, I must leave my son. I
don't have time to date you. Dating you takes time
away from looking for a job. I want to put all my
time into finding a job instead of leaving him." His
eyes became dark, I assumed due to the room being
dimly lit. The first time I saw his rage, I was dizzy
not understanding how a moment ago everything
seemed great.

"When I left for the military rotation," he
continued, "it was voluntary. They didn't make me
go. I left because I didn't have a job."

"I thought they said you had to go. I didn't
know." I had tears in my eyes that I couldn't stop
from flowing down my face.

"How would you know anything?" he yelled
back at me. "I have the opportunity to do contract

work which will pay me over $200,000 a year." He was sitting higher on the sofa as if he had grown several inches…his eyes even darker…looking down at me. "I'll do anything not to leave my son. But if I must go, at least I can make enough money to buy a house with cash."

With a defeated voice, I asked, "Is there some date you have planned to leave if you don't find a job?"

"They want me there by February," he said as he sat back on the sofa seeming to lose those extra inches in height as he lowered his voice.

"Under three months from now," I whispered feeling this night was surreal to me just as the airport return had been surreal to him.

"If I take time to stay with you, instead of looking for a job, I may have to leave my son. I had advice from a religious leader that I should end everything with you."

Cast aside by the man I loved…my tears moved into a pouring storm. I descended into my first desperate plea with him. "You can take whatever time you need to find a job. Just don't end things with me. I love you." I said it. I said the words that must have a different meaning from any other man I had known because the words felt different. My love for him brought in a light. A

•

purpose. A completeness.

"You love me?" he asked. "I can't say I'm there with you on love."

This is from a man who had said he wanted marriage with me. My telling him I love him and that he could take all the time he needs to find a job was letting him know I would put up with bad behavior…very bad behavior.

Agreeing to slavery, I sat on the floor at his feet crying. "I'll see you when you have time."

"You aren't hearing me," he raged on. "I won't stay with you wasting my time when I need to get a job. Wasting my time with you means that I will go overseas and leave my son."

On the floor leaning on his legs, his jeans became wet with my storm of tears. "I'll see you whenever you're free," I said. "You eat right? When you take a break from any job search, I'll be there."

"You'll be here for me?" he asked his voice becoming soft again as he quickly wavered between compassion and rage.

"Yes," I declared shaking…many times shaking because of him as I seemed to be making contracts or vows to be there no matter what. "I'll be here for you always…forever."

Bobby reached down forcefully and pulled me up to his lap. He kissed my wet face and pressed his cheek hard against mine as he had done before. "I'll stay with you," he said, "I am falling for you. I just can't say the words."

"Why can't you?"

"I don't know. I just can't."

He held me for a long time. I stopped crying feeling dehydrated and exhausted as if all the fluids in my body were gone. Desperate to not have him leave me again, I gave him all my power that night and many other nights to come…the giving of my life and even my soul.

I had never allowed this type of relationship to be in my life as an adult. My mother moved between the extremes of what seemed like unconditional love to a cold narcissist. Being a child, I was forced to be in the cage my mother created. The cage with Bobby is the cage I allowed being that I'm an adult. Or did I never leave the cage my mother built? Either way, I gave him the key to my cage.

•

COLORADO HELL

OVER THE NEXT FEW WEEKS, we spent time together most evenings after I was free from work. All the time with him was not expected after his declaration that time had to be put into the job search.

My friend, Sara, set Bobby up for an interview with her husband's business, but she told me that Bobby acted odd during the interview. She said he mentioned me to her husband and said he had no long-term plans with me. Sara said that her husband wondered why Bobby mentioned me during an interview. Her husband also said Bobby seemed overly confident and acted as if he didn't care whether he was offered the job. Despite being qualified, Bobby didn't receive a job offer.

Christmas was coming, and Bobby discussed a trip with our children over the holidays. "Chuck wants to go to Colorado," Bobby said.

At the time, I didn't know the power Chuck exerted over Bobby. The power was not compared to one umbilical cord that a mother will not release, but instead a hundred unhealthy cords connected to Bobby, making him a puppet to his son. Throughout my relationship with Bobby, Chuck chose our vacation locations, restaurants, and activities...this wasn't normal.

"I would have liked a Caribbean Island with you," Bobby continued, "but you acted like I was going to murder you and leave you in some foreign country when I mentioned going away alone."

"I didn't think that. You just caught me off guard. I would love to be alone on an island with you."

As if I said nothing, he continued talking about Colorado. He must have already told his son we would all go to Colorado. Bobby was in charge.

He then stated, "I don't even like the cold." Chuck was also in charge.

We continued to plan the Colorado trip

discussing cities to visit and activities to do. I told him that my niece and a close friend lived there.

"How much money for my part," I asked while looking at plane tickets and hotels.

"Nothing," he firmly said pulling out his credit card. "I'm paying for everything." Even throughout our friendship, he was always grabbing the bill as if he was the kind of man to financially take care of things, being the grounding force, creating safety and security.

Our trip was planned with us returning on Christmas day because Bobby made plans for us to be with his friends that evening. My dad, the main person in my family I was close to, had passed away years before. So, I was agreeable to not spending time with the rest of my family that season.

After Bobby booked the trip, I began planning for the cold winter outdoor activities. During my time in the military, I had lived in Germany where I learned about layering clothing, wearing hats, gloves, and warm boots to stay warm. My daughter, who was a young teen at the time, had an attitude about wearing long johns until we arrived. Then she was glad to have them.

I spoke to my close friend, James, who lived in Colorado before Bobby finalized the plane tickets. James said since he had a company car to drive, we could borrow his personal car while we were there.

When we arrived at the airport, James picked us up. We dropped James at his house and started our adventure…our first trip together. We planned to end the trip with a hot springs activity with James and his family, and we would then return his car.

The first activity was a two-hour horseback ride through the Garden of the Gods. I felt at home on horses even though I didn't ride them often. My family owned a cattle ranch until I was ten years old, and we had horses. I started with a pony and graduated to my Appaloosa horse. When we moved to town, we didn't have my horse anymore. Having a few friends with horses, I rode occasionally over the years.

Bobby never spoke of riding, and he always lived in a city. Yet, when at the Garden of the Gods, he told the horse keepers he was an expert rider. Bobby's personality changed to being arrogant when on the horse. I had ridden in Steamboat Springs, Colorado on a trip with my dad when he was working for Zig Zigler. I knew the drill to get in a single line behind the guide.

Bobby quickly went up to being second,

right behind the guide. His son was last. As a mom, I would have been behind my kids to ensure they were safe. That is why I had my daughter in front of me. Those one hundred cords to Chuck were not always attached when Bobby just thought of Bobby. He held his head high while on the horse and never looked back at us for the two-hour ride.

The Garden of the Gods had a relaxing energy and a beauty I had not seen before. The horses had more courage than I did going up and down steep areas of the mountains. When I was sixteen, I took flying lessons for a private pilot's license. I had no fear when "buzzing the boats" along the Florida coast where I grew up. I rode my motorcycle with no helmet and drove my Grand Torino at speeds over 100 mph down I-95. I was fearless and reckless, but having a child grounded me into the reality that she needed me to be alive. Being a mother allowed fear to creep into everything including the possibility of the horses slipping on the rocky trail.

Despite my nerves, I generally relaxed into a different state when on the horse. I've dreamed of riding, and now I believe those dreams are memories of other lifetimes.

My daughter's favorite activity was the horseback ride. My favorite was the snow tubing a couple of days later. The first time down sent me into that same sense of fear where: *I must stay alive and healthy for my child.* Every other time sliding down the snow was a thrill that radiated through my body.

Toward the end of the trip, we came close to having sex, but we didn't. It was passionate to be with him for the first time with his clothes off and him rubbing me with my wearing only a thong. I couldn't remember in my entire life wanting someone so badly. But he made a strange comment to me that if we had sex, we were going to go down the road of breaking up versus not having sex before marriage and then going down the road of getting married.

Bobby had a "1950s white picket fence" idea of how relationships should progress even though we both had sexual relationships in the past. I thought to myself that if he wanted the white picket fence, and since he was talking about marriage, I would go along with his sexual boundaries.

Our trip was ruined by one of Bobby's irrational explosions. We went to a sandwich restaurant that offered a sandwich and soup combo meal. Three times a day he wanted to eat out in between constant activities. Everything with Bobby seemed like an overindulgence during the trip and always.

After a heavy breakfast, I was not very hungry. His son and I were off to the side talking about the menu where we decided Chuck would have a sandwich, and I would have his soup. When trying to order, Bobby became confused since I was ordering for his son even though I explained Chuck and I were sharing a meal. The ordering took a long time due to Bobby's strange confusion. Even years later, Bobby would mention the restaurant order as me being controlling.

For the rest of the day, Bobby was quiet. He couldn't hide the look on his face when he went dark because something took control. He became a different person.

That night, once the kids were in bed, he catapulted into repeating the restaurant expcricncc while yelling. I seriously considered flying home the next day because I felt so tightly enclosed in the cage when I was stuck in a hotel room with his anger. I thought through everything in my head before deciding to stay. If we left, that would ruin the trip for my daughter. Plus, it was right before Christmas. Leaving would be quite a blemish over the holidays for her.

Things stayed tense with minimum talking

and no touching. On the day of our hot springs activity at the end of our trip, my friend met us with his girlfriend and their two girls. My daughter was close to their age. We all changed into our bathing suits and met at the hot springs.

In the water, my friend was wrapped around his girlfriend the whole time acting the way people in love act. My daughter was with the other two girls. Bobby was with his son. I was alone in the water.

Bobby's theme of passive-aggressive behavior repeated many times through the years, but that was always better than his explosive rage. My solution through the years became usually walking silently on eggshells, instead of engaging in any of his attempts to argue. This is how my dad dealt with my mother. Otherwise, the arguments were even more emotionally exhausting because these people can't be reasoned with. In their world, it's never their fault.

Arriving home on Christmas day and leaving the airport, we walked to my SUV. We drove in my SUV to the airport because I had space for all our luggage. When we went to leave the parking garage, I was fatigued, not only physically from the trip but emotionally from being with this angry, passive-aggressive man. I asked him to drive.

•

That left him in the driver's seat to pay for the parking garage. As he entered the area to pay, I took out my wallet because it was my SUV.

Bobby pulled out his credit card and made one of his cold comments as he paid. "Good news kids. For New Year's Angie is taking us to Hawaii."

He must have resented paying for not only the parking but for the trip as well even though before we
left, he insisted on paying for everything.

The trip was hell. Merry Christmas to me.

ALONE...AGAIN

AFTER CHRISTMAS I WENT back to teaching after the New Year. Bobby continued to have time to see me. He did not mention job searches. Obviously, he would be leaving soon for the contract work overseas. Part of his plan to leave involved Bobby asking if I could take his son to a church group one evening a week while he was gone. I was glad he included me in what I viewed as a stepmother role. He viewed this as someone taking his child to a church group. That ended up being a hassle. I had to rush home from work, feed Chuck, rush to the church group, and rush his son back home. A few times Chuck didn't go to school saying he was sick leaving me to show up at their house with Chuck not there. Then I would take a long drive to his mom's work to pick him up causing us to be late. My lack of boundaries with Bobby extended to Chuck and his mom with me allowing the whole group to be inconsiderate.

Days before leaving, Bobby still held on to his beliefs that we would not have sex before marriage. Bobby was saying more about possible dates to marry each other all the while he knew he was leaving the country for a year of contract work in Afghanistan. We had come to the point where we were doing everything except having intercourse. He had professed his love for me saying he had never really loved anyone. Many days we would spend hours holding each other, laughing, talking, and making each other come with our hands and mouths.

Bobby left. He flew back to the war zone, and my heart broke again. We went back to Skype and emails. Our emails must have been like wartime love letters of past wars…love letters that were not instant emails but handwritten by wives and girlfriends…many not received by fallen soldiers.

BEACH HELL

BOBBY WAS APPROVED FOR a vacation after being in the contractor job for five months. He rented a beach house for us in a small beach town an hour from my house. I picked him up from the airport, and we hugged for so long that it seemed we were permanently intertwined as one.

The next day we drove separate cars to the beach because I was going to drive my daughter back before the end of the trip due to her summer camp. During the drive, my daughter and I discussed how I grew up near the beach in South Florida. I loved everything about the beach. The view, the sound, the smell…I even loved the sand in everything especially between my toes as I felt the warm sand.

Arriving at the beach, the house was on two lots right on the beach. The house was one story up on stilts with an open area under the house for barbecuing and relaxing. Inside, windows covered the living room wall bringing in the beach view. The master bedroom was downstairs. Bobby suddenly complained about his knee hurting, saying he wanted to stay in the master bedroom.

My daughter and I would be sharing a room upstairs, and Chuck would have a room upstairs to himself. The three of us upstairs would share a bathroom. King Bobby would have a bathroom to himself downstairs. This is not how I would arrange the room choices.

Besides that, I liked the house. Bobby didn't. He complained about the high ceiling wasting electricity. Why did it matter? He was paying a flat rate. He complained that the place was old. I saw it as being updated. With those complaints and others, it seemed Bobby wanted to be in a mansion.

The house was rented for a week during the Fourth of July, and Bobby told me he was open to me inviting friends to come out. He did say he wanted to spend the fourth alone with the kids and me. On July the third, Bobby was on the phone with a friend. Someone he had not mentioned to me before. When he got off the phone, he said his friend and his wife were coming that day and said they would be staying with us. I immediately thought about the next day being the Fourth of July, the day he wanted to be alone with the kids and me. I was open to meeting new people, but he changed what he said. Besides, he would be leaving back to Afghanistan in a few days. I wanted time alone with him.

Bobby's friends arrived in time to start cooking dinner. The wife, who clearly did not want to be there, stayed with me cutting vegetables in the house, while Bobby and his friend were downstairs grilling meat. Once the food was ready, we ate together with Bobby and his friend doing most of the talking to each other. The wife did not talk except for small things like, "Please pass the salt."

The friend and his wife went to bed early in Bobby's room, and I confronted Bobby. I still had not learned confronting the master was a battle to worsen things.

Bobby and I finished cleaning the kitchen. Our kids had gone upstairs…his son to spend hours on his gaming addiction…my daughter to read and

.

text. Bobby went to relax on the small sofa with his feet up taking up most of the space. I thought of sitting at the end of the sofa, but he was acting odd.

"It seems your friends will be with us tomorrow night for the Fourth of July," I said.

"Yeah. It seems so."

"His wife is quiet almost as if she is pissed," I said trying to figure out her attitude. I didn't like being stuck with her, a stranger, preparing food with her hardly saying a word.

"They have a shitty marriage. I told him that no matter what, don't divorce her. If he does, he'll see his kids every other weekend like I am with Chuck. My biggest regret in life is leaving Chuck's mom."

I wasn't sure how to take that. Was it just about Chuck or something about his mom as well? Either way, at that moment, I wasn't interested in spending time with his angry friends when Bobby would be leaving soon.

"You said you wanted to spend the Fourth of July alone with the kids and me that the other days didn't matter as far as having friends or family down here."

As if he shape-shifted into an animal, he jumped to a squatting position on the sofa. I jumped myself out of fear. "I never said that, and I think," he said with sarcasm in his loud voice, "since I'm the one who paid for the place, and since I'm the one overseas working my ass off, I'll have people here whenever I want."

He continued with his voice becoming louder. I didn't say anything back because I did not know what to say as his words made less and less sense. Bobby rambled on and repeated himself. It was another night of an exhausting argument. I was almost in a trance when I snapped to realizing I had met him at the coast with us driving in separate cars. I walked out while he was still yelling. I went upstairs where I was staying with my daughter and locked the door behind me because I was scared. He was taken over by something else…again.

My daughter had fallen asleep. I packed our things and waited for Bobby to go to his bedroom downstairs. I woke my daughter up and we left.

The next day my daughter asked what happened. I said I needed to pick up some medicine from home because I was not feeling well. She pushed a bit knowing I never become sick besides an occasional headache. She was old enough to know something was wrong between Bobby and me. But she gave up asking why.

The morning of the Fourth of July, Bobby and I talked on the phone as if nothing had happened, and I drove back before dinner time. His friends had left.

The beach was crowded, but Bobby wanted to be where he could put his feet in the water while watching the fireworks. That sounded nice.

We walked along the boardwalk where there were street vendors. He bought Chuck a fake sword with colored lights. I found out in another argument that Bobby did not like me "taking over" as he called it telling his son what to do. I felt that telling both kids things like, "Hurry up. We're leaving," was normal, but apparently not.

Chuck started waving the fake sword close to my daughter's face and my face while Bobby said nothing. This went on long enough, and I was shocked Bobby just stood there.

I had to stop the kid. My kid was involved. I found out from picking Chuck up for several months every week for that pain-in-the-ass church night, that the kid listened to me, but not his parents. Both parents let Chuck run things. Being that I was a teacher, I saw life with kids as simple. Be consistent. Be the parent.

"Chuck," I said sternly, "If you hit her or me with that sword, I will take it and you won't get it back."

He stopped. It seemed Bobby would let that

spoiled brat hit one of us in the face. Of course, the behavior was not Chuck's fault. It was poor parenting.

The next day, Bobby rented two jet skis for the four of us to take turns. I've been on jet skis in lakes, but not in the ocean. I prefer the calmness of an early morning glassy lake before the boats are out--similar to the best time to water ski.

Fighting the ocean waves was a task. One wave hit me hard and something hit one of my eyes. I road back to shore and gave up the jet ski to Bobby who had been waiting. "My eye is killing me. Something hit me."

He looked at me, his eyes going dark. "You look fine," he said as he took the jet ski.

I sat on the shore not knowing what to do. His son was there with me waiting for my daughter to come in from her turn. The pain was terrible.

When my daughter came to shore, I was crying. His son went out on the jet ski she was on. Bobby had left his bag with his car keys on our towels. My daughter and I went to the car to get into the water cooler so I could try putting ice on my eye. Besides the ice, I flushed my eye with water. We arrived back at the shore while Bobby was coming in on his jet ski.

He immediately started yelling at me from a

•

long distance away. "Where did you go? I was riding in and didn't see you." More irrational behavior instead of asking me about my eye.

"We were here at our towels before you got back to shore," I said as I stood there with a half-frozen water bottle against my eye, which I saw in the car mirror was red.

He was distracted from yelling at me by the man who rented us the jet skis. "It's past time. Can you get your kid into shore."

Bobby began to frantically wave at his son who was far out from shore. Here they were, late as usual. Inconsiderate as usual.

"What do we want to do next," Bobby asked as Chuck got off the jet ski. The jet ski rental man took the jet ski and gave Bobby an annoyed look then looked at his watch.

"I want to swim here at this beach," Chuck said.

Normally, I would let King Chuck or Master Bobby decide. But I had to decide what to do about my eye. "I need to get inside the house and have a closer look at my eye so I can figure out what to do. There's a beach at the house to swim at as well."

Bobby was standing there in a weird position I had seen before. He looked how I imagined a lizard would look if it were standing up on its back legs. He was hunched over with his arms and hands not at his sides, almost looking double-jointed. Even in the bright sunlight, his blue eyes looked dark. At that moment, I said what I needed, which was to go back to the house. I wish I had taken control of my life and my daughter's life all the time with these reptilian soul suckers instead of just when in pain and when swords were flying at us.

Back at the house, I laid down and flushed my eye with more water. My daughter asked several times if I needed to go to urgent care…a question I would expect from Bobby.

I was back to normal within a couple of hours. That night Bobby said he thought I was faking it trying to ruin the day. What a crazy statement. Why would I do that? We had our kids to think of which caused me to put on a happy face no matter how he acted.

I had never had anyone take my pain and say something like that. He never asked if I was still in pain or what he could do to help.

•

BACK TO AFGHANISTAN

BOBBY LEFT FOR AFGHANISTAN a few days after the beach trip. Even though it was hard to see him go, the beach trip was worse than Colorado. My head spun from the love bombing at the beginning of our relationship to the darkness that emerged at the beach. As I looked back to the beginning when it seemed I had found the one, his beast was hibernating like a bear would hibernate in the winter. Unlike the bear, who would hibernate all winter, his beast would come out any time.

A couple of weeks after Bobby left to finish his last six months, he hit me out of nowhere with another relationship-altering decision. He had been gone for the six-month military tour and had finished six months as a contractor. He was supposed to come home in six months. When he signed up for this contract job, he promised me he would stay with this work for only one year making it all together one-and-one-half years away.

Getting onto Skype I wasn't fed any of the sweet talk. Bobby was quick and direct. "I've decided to stay here in the contract work longer than I planned. If I come home in six months, I won't have enough money."

"You're doing what?" I asked, caught completely by surprise.

"The money here is too good to leave. I don't have a job lined up for when I return."

Then I confronted him with the facts of what he had said. He never liked his own words being thrown at him. "You promised you were coming back six months from now. You said this was it."

Challenging Bobby, I had woken the beast. "You don't understand," he yelled going from calm to rage in an instant. "You don't care about Chuck and me and what we need. You sit there in your high-need job in your perfect life where things are easy."

The attack on me, opened a rare comment back to the beast, "Yeah. I had it easy. Poor family. Put myself through college after the military. I've had a gun pointed at me twice. This and more trauma you seem to have forgotten… easy life for sure."

Even though he knew my true story, Bobby had created an untrue story about me in his world.

He went on talking like he didn't hear me as he typically did. "I'm staying longer, and I won't ever ask your opinion again about finances for me and my son."

"You aren't asking me now. You're telling me."

He became more enraged. "I can't believe you don't understand."

"I understand that you were going to be gone six months. Then you were going to be gone a year for contract work. You promised that was it. You're breaking your promise."

He continued to yell. I stopped talking as I finished contributing to his endless cycle of repeating the same thing. I had fought back more than normal which left me drained of energy. I would feel the same if Bobby put an IV in my arm and drained my blood to a state of near-death…keeping me alive to repeat the cycle… build me up a bit…take me back to hell.

Being upstairs in my study, I looked out my French doors at the blooming crêpe myrtles. When in this pit with him, instead of seeing the beauty around me, I can't see or feel anything except death.

He ran out of steam and said, "Do you remember what you said about staying mad? You said your grandmother told you to never go to bed mad."

My physical body was immobilized. I was glued there looking at his strange face on the computer.

"We can Skype tomorrow," he said softly as some color returned to his dark eyes.

I agreed so I could get off Skype and be done with him forever. At that point, I cried in this relationship more than in all my other relationships.

My daughter, who spent most of her time with friends, was home upset over a break-up. I bought tickets for a movie to be with my daughter but not with my daughter. She needed some distraction, and I needed the movie to be vicarious even if just for two hours. I feel I lost important years with her because I was usually in a state of

●

Twin Flame trauma, a zombie state of living, yet not living.

The next day, I saw that Bobby tried to Skype with me. A few days later, I sent him a short email that our relationship was over. No response.

Within two weeks, it was as if the light switch was back on for me. I emailed that I loved him. I left Skype messages. Still—no response. Having him overseas, I couldn't simply drive over to him. I wouldn't know if or when he would return.

THANKSGIVING ...NOT THANKFUL

AFTER THE LIGHT SWITCH came back on for me and he didn't respond to me reaching out, I went on with my life. We had broken up in September and Thanksgiving was coming up. For a couple of years, I had the hobby of dancing—waltz, west coast, two-step, and nightclub. Bobby never went with me. I had friends in the dance community, and I dated men there soon after Bobby and I broke up.

During the week of Thanksgiving, I made plans with a man I had gone out with a few times. We would attend a party at one of my friend's homes. The man met me at my house, and we drove in my car to my friend's place since I knew the neighborhood where she lived.

Unknown to me, Bobby had flown home from Afghanistan for Thanksgiving. I picked up his mail at a post office box the entire time he was gone.

On the night of my friend's party, Bobby sent me a text about his mail: "I appreciate you picking up my mail despite how our relationship ended. I want to come over tonight and get my mail."

I was surprised. I kept going to the post office once a week without planning how to get the mail to him. The energy between us that was dissipating, started to rise as I responded in text: "I won't be home tonight. I can get it to you tomorrow."

The beast awoke out of nowhere after being so polite. "I need my mail tonight. You can't keep my mail from me. I need it now."

Like old times, he was demanding total control and made comments that had no justification. I sent another text: "I'm not keeping your mail from you. Like I said, I have plans. I will get it to you tomorrow."

More texts: "I need it today. What time can you leave it outside for me?"

"I'm out. I won't be home until late. You'll get it tomorrow." The situation became worse with his demented side.

My plans continued with the other man leaving his car at my house. We drove my car to my friend's party. My daughter texted me while I was at the party that Bobby had come by my house asking for his mail.

Coming by after I said no. Speaking to my daughter while he was angry. Ringing the doorbell when a car he wouldn't recognize was in the driveway. This was all a higher level of insanity and control.

I sent him a scathing text message after that. "My daughter just texted me. As I said, I am not home to give you the mail. It is not allowable to show up at my home and talk to my underaged daughter when you are angry. You are not welcome at my home. I will contact one of our friends tomorrow about leaving your mail with them.

If Bobby had any true sense of urgency with his mail, he could have contacted me before leaving Afghanistan to give a date he would be in town for his mail. Despite the breakup, I would have been willing to meet on a day convenient to him because I knew he would have limited time on his vacation. However, his showing up at my house left me symbolically shielding around my house with my text to him.

I called our mutual friend, Sarah, to set up leaving his mail with her. Walking into her house, she shook her head and hugged me. "If he's been mean to you, I'll have my husband talk to him," she said compassionately.

"He demanded I drop everything and give him his mail immediately even though it's been sitting around for months. That's strange behavior."

"Mail that's collected cobwebs can always wait one to two days. It's a rule." Her joke made us both laugh.

After another day passed, I fell back into the strange connection with Bobby. I texted and called him. He didn't respond. My longing increased, but he was out of reach again…physically and emotionally.

I moved on by dating the new guy…and moved on by having sex with him. It had been a while because I was dating the Virgin Mother form of Bobby. I became bored with the new guy's attitude…the attitude that had some similarities to

Bobby. So, I moved on to another man. And then another.

Occasionally, I thought of Bobby for the first year away from him. There were times when I felt devastated. Even after all the arguments, I wanted him back. I reached out occasionally not hearing back. I stared at pictures and poured through past emails where we had professed our love to each other. I cried while listening to songs that made me think of him. Bobby was gone.

The next year, it was as if the light switch turned off completely. After two years free, he became the same as other men from my past— locked in a mass grave in the back of my mind.

I was no longer Bobby's slave living under his control and abuse. The men I dated were supportive and respectful. We laughed. We had sex. I had normal in my life again.

Then I ran into Bobby. The light switch I thought was permanently off switched on. When I saw Bobby, all my loving feelings flooded back.

•

LIGHTING THE FIRE

WHEN WE FIRST BROKE up, I started to see a counselor once a month. The counselor and I talked occasionally about Bobby. I mainly focused on finding myself again after losing who I was. With Bobby, my life became his life. I didn't make restaurant choices when I was with him. Either Bobby or Chuck would choose any activities. I was his Stepford wife.

At the counselor's, I was leaving late one day because she asked to keep me late to share a story about herself. I was making my plan to leave teaching to finish my doctorate, and the counselor had some personal information that correlated with my plans. She shared her story. Bobby was in the waiting area when I walked out of her door. There he was in the country, and at this therapist's office that I only visited once a month. It was like that cliché: *I've seen a ghost.*

His therapist opened the door and Bobby said, "This is Angie."

Without hesitating, I walked over and hugged him. He hugged me as well.

Bobby said, "It's nice to see you." Then he walked into his therapist's office. There was nothing I could do besides watch him walk away.

With my summer teaching schedule as being off on vacation, I was free for the rest of the day. Getting into my new Mustang, I decided to wait for him…if he would be willing to talk to me.

He had sold his car before leaving for Afghanistan, so I didn't know what car he drove. He walked out to a Toyota Highlander. That was strange to me because I almost bought a Toyota Highlander the year before but at the last minute, I

●

decided to get a sports car when a friend was talking about buying a sports car.

I walked up to him. He smiled and laughed as he asked me to lunch. Here Bobby was in front of me after two years, and a cherry on top with him asking me to go to lunch.

That was not the first time we ran into each other. Through the years, we would run into each other about once a year somewhere in town. Once we ran into each other at a dog shelter, a shelter neither of us had ever been to. There was always some energy pulling us back together into a bubble where we would interact.

We went for lunch and then stood outside talking. I looked down at his body imagining him naked. I snapped back into the reality that we were standing outside in the summer sun, not in my bedroom, as he told me to confront him with anything I wanted to say. Free from my slavery, that was the first day I was allowed to say everything. He listened.

After my venting, Bobby told me he would like to get together for coffee or do something in a few days. We met at a bookstore. While staring into his eyes, the familiar fire ignited inside of me. I had just begun dating someone. The relationship was going downhill because he had similar personality traits to Bobby such as becoming angry for no apparent reason.

I generally wouldn't argue with the guy. Instead, allowing him to spin off in his anger, he would run out of fuel, and we would continue our relationship. The difference between Bobby and this new guy was that I didn't care. The new guy could rage on with my only reaction being to look at my watch…wondering when he would be done so we could continue having fun or having sex. Any depth wasn't there for me.

At the bookstore, Bobby told me he was about to leave for a short military rotation of four months and then would be retiring. Disappointed to hear this, I felt we could be moving back into something…friendship…maybe the potential of something more, and he was leaving. Only four months. I thought maybe he was finally in a place where he would come home and choose me instead of choosing money. I was falling back into my programming to keep hoping…keep waiting.

He said he would return by the beginning of March. I was on the rodeo committee, which meant it was free for us to attend any concert when he returned. George Strait and other popular performers were on the concert lineup. When I explained all of this, Bobby seemed excited about

•

attending a concert and said he would contact me when he returned.

To not be an ass by breaking up with the man I was dating right before Valentine's Day, I decided to stay with him. There was also a need inside of me to stay because I didn't want to be alone when Bobby came back. I was trying to protect my heart from jumping back in with Bobby. A few days after Valentine's Day, I broke things off with the man I had been dating. I couldn't deal with the man's anger any longer. I was able to let go of him due to his crazy rage while holding on to Bobby for years. Bobby had a hold on me that no one else had.

I contacted Bobby the first week of March, and he was back from his military rotation. He didn't contact me like he said he would. Lady Antebellum was a group from the rodeo concert lineup he wanted to see.

Warmth returned to my life knowing I would see him within days. On concert night, we met about 15 minutes from my house because he was running late. Reluctantly, I left my car parked in a restaurant parking lot with his reassurance my car would be fine while we were gone.

Once we arrived at the rodeo, Bobby was constantly touching the small of my back, hugging me, touching my leg....it was an overload of energy.

Touching my hair he said, "I can't believe you're here with me."

Those casual touches went on all through the rodeo. Before the concert started, we went to the concession stands. In a joking manner, I mentioned the constant touching. After that, the touching stopped, and he even turned his body slightly away from me when we sat back down to listen to the concert.

We left the rodeo and drove back to the restaurant where I had left my car. Bobby dropped me off in the dark parking lot not even watching that I was safe inside my car before he drove off.

His hands were all over me. Then a cold shutdown. In my confusion, I called him. "I feel like it would have been nice if you had kissed me tonight." He could reject me. He had before. I had nothing to lose.

He paused for what seemed like forever. Then Bobby finally replied. "Wow. A kiss. That would be really nice."

I was breathless.

"Come over right now then...and kiss me."

"Okay."

•

During the few minutes it took to get to my house, I was full of the Twin Flame energy, or in truth, I was high on alien deception that was buried in my programming. I felt Bobby was finally home and back with me...us...there will be an us again.

As soon as Bobby came through the door, we kissed. We were back to that PG-rated kissing. Then his hands were all over me.

Abruptly, he shut down the energy. "I can't do this with you. I want to date other people," he continued. "I didn't get to date anybody since you."

I assumed that he had seen prostitutes overseas because he talked to me about that kind of thing. Any other man speaking of prostitutes, and I would be disgusted. With Bobby, I accepted everything unconditionally.

Back into slavery, I said, "I don't care if you date other people. I want to date you." I allowed him to run the relationship, run my life, and essentially, be disrespectful to me. He would be dating women while I was starting to feel love again. He had the choice to put me back in the cage.

"I can't do that to you," he said. "I could do that to other women. But I can't date you and them."

I assumed he didn't want to date me because our relationship was difficult when we dated before.

We went back to being friends with my longing for Bobby coming and going. The aliens were turning my light switch on and off like some cruel game they played with our hearts.

We went out as friends about once a week for a few years. I dated men, but he never talked about anyone he dated. There was one man I dated I could see a future with.

My relationship with him was foreign compared to what I had with Bobby. This man had no anger towards me. Disagreements were resolved respectfully talking through any issues. Mr. Respectful was spiritual. He was opening me up to spiritual beliefs that I had not connected with, which helped me to move into hypnosis and energy work.

One complaint was that Mr. Respectful only saw me once a week. Bobby started asking me to get together a couple of times a week causing me to feel Bobby was sending a subliminal message such as: *Hey look at me. I'm here. I'm available more often than he is. Choose me.*

There were a lot of changes going on in my life. I had left teaching and started my business in hypnosis and energy clearing. New friends entered my life as old friends left because I was changing. Between Mr. Respectful and my new life, there

•

wasn't much time to see Bobby.

My new job in spiritual work helped me to connect with my high self in a way that I usually felt I didn't need Bobby. I was walking in the clouds. Humans can't stay in the clouds forever. Earth must change as well. During this awakening time, I was back and forth…up and down.

One night, Mr. Respectful ended our relationship. Crying, I contacted Bobby. He came over and held me for hours saying everything I needed to hear including that I deserved more from a man than what I was getting. He focused on Mr. Respectful not being available to be supportive and loving.

Bobby pulled me over onto his lap as if he was coming onto me, but I was so distraught by the other man that I couldn't feel anything except pain. He held me in an awkward embrace that night while I did realize the truth in what Bobby was saying: Mr. Respectful was not the man for me.

BEATING A MAN

LIFE WENT ON WITHOUT Mr. Respectful. I filled part of my empty heart by spending time with Bobby. There were "dark nights of the soul," running my business, and juggling new friends as I released the last of my old friends. When dating Bobby, I was confused regarding him and me. This spiritual chapter in my life involved me being confused about myself. What added to that confusion was the occasional pull towards the attraction between Bobby and me…the attraction I couldn't control. The aliens had me by the invisible puppet strings as I went between feeling I had a path to help the world to my life spiraling down as I focused on Bobby.

Since I wasn't dating him anymore, I generally didn't experience his rage directed towards me. However, being in a car with him tended to awaken the beast. I had seen him drive at speeds well over the speed limit and tail right behind cars in the left lane. His reasoning was, "They shouldn't be in the left lane. It's the passing lane."

We were leaving my house one day when I asked about his son's mom. They had been apart for years, but she acted odd towards me on the rare occasions I saw her.

"Did anything ever happen between you and Chuck's mom when you stayed with her after coming home from Afghanistan," I asked.

The beast wokc that day as he yelled, "I would never fuck that fat and ugly woman."

Not knowing where the rage was coming from, I didn't respond. It was a question that didn't involve me personally because we weren't involved in a relationship at that time. I was only curious since Chuck's mom was silent whenever she saw me as if I wasn't there…no hello, goodbye, or even eye contact. Whereas, when Bobby was out of the country, and I was taking her child to and from the church group every week for six months, she was friendly.

Nothing else was spoken as he drove onto the highway and headed a few miles toward our destination. Bobby began speeding and swerving in and out between other vehicles. He was chasing someone with both cars taking turns being in the lead as if we were on a racetrack.

After miles of holding on to my seat in fear of my own life, Bobby exited onto the feeder road and pulled into a strip mall with the other car close behind. He parked and practically jumped out of the car as did the people in the other car, two men near Bobby's size and a woman.

Rushing towards the driver, Bobby took the first punch. I stayed in the car, locked the door, and climbed into the driver's seat thinking there was no way I would let Bobby drive us after that road rage incident. Bobby and the driver threw punch after punch beating each other.

The man not involved in the fight came to where I was sitting. "Can you come and get your husband?"

I said nothing. I wasn't moving from the locked car for fear of someone pulling out a gun because I had already been involved in gun incidents due to robberies and safety threats towards

.

me. Bobby had a hold over me, but I wasn't going to put myself naked inside the lion's den by becoming involved in his fight.

When it seemed, no one won the road rage fight, the two juvenile-acting men returned to their cars. I unlocked Bobby's car long enough for him to get in and drove away before he could put his seatbelt on.

Adrenaline flying, Bobby said, "That felt so good."

I drove back to my house in silence. Once there, I said I needed to go and went inside alone. Bobby just said a loud, "Whatever."

The next day, Bobby showed up at my house with a black eye and bruising on his forehead. His knuckles from the day before had swelled and scabbed over.

"It reality sunk in today how stupid I was yesterday," he said.

I just listened. Saying anything could wake the beast.

"I don't know what gets into me sometimes," he continued.

Still, I'm silent.

"I told Chuck I fell on my mountain bike."

That was a good excuse. He must be familiar with making excuses to cover his insanity.

"Will you tell your daughter I fell on my bike?" he asked.

"Sure," I said softly, still feeling the trauma of seeing the fight and fearing for my safety.

Later, he would blame me for the fight stating I said something that pissed him off. That must have been me asking whether he had sex with his son's mom years after they were together. She's not "fat and ugly" as he described her. I would describe her as attractive, bubbly, and smart. In his world, everything is different.

A psychic friend did tell me she saw a vision of them in bed together years after the break-up. I psychically heard a conversation where she asked him to get back together with her. Sometime after that Bobby said she had asked him to reunite. That would explain her silence towards me.

After his bruising healed, he accused me of telling my daughter about him beating a random man during road rage. Due to my shame of being with a man like him, I never admitted to anyone, especially my daughter, that I stayed with him. Even after that event, my choosing to be in the car with Bobby, showed something else was controlling me.

US AGAIN

My OLDER SISTER HAD brain cancer. My daughter and I flew out of state to see her several times after her diagnosis the year before. She went into remission, then the cancer took over to the point of a quick death. My daughter and I left the state for a couple of weeks to spend time with our family and to attend the funeral. I didn't tell Bobby I was leaving.

Bobby called me while we were at my sister's home with her husband and in-laws. He asked why he was finding out on Facebook instead of me calling him. I had moments of lucidity such as knowing he wasn't a boyfriend...why take time to contact him? With my sister and my dad gone, there was no more unconditional love and support. No more private family jokes.

Soon after I returned from the funeral, Bobby came over and took me to a pond that had a long bridge crossing over the pond. We took bread because the pond is full of turtles. After feeding the turtles, as a joke, I mooned him.

Rushing up behind me, he grabbed me. "I like seeing your ass...touching it is even better."

It had been years since his hands had been on me like that. If any other friend had touched me like that, I would have slapped him. With Bobby, all things in life were different. I turned around to try to kiss him, and he said no.

After that things were changing with us becoming an "us" again although he was still cold. We spent many nights running our hands all over our bodies bringing each other to the point of climax. But he wouldn't kiss me. "Kissing would mean a commitment," he said.

To me, a kiss should come before his hands were all over me.

On November 11th, everything changed with him kissing me. Considering I was so deeply under the Twin Flame spell, I saw it as a synchronicity of the numbers: 11 and 11.

I thought back to years before when he discussed marrying me on synchronous dates like 10/10, 11/11, or 12/12. I started seeing those synchronous numbers often, especially when I thought of Bobby.

When attending a meditation an energy healer was leading, someone mentioned she was marrying her Twin Flame. That was the night I learned the word for our relationship. It made sense then why I felt the way I did for years. After that, I kept hearing about Twin Flames. I became obsessed with Twin Flame videos, books, and blogs as I completely bought into the bullshit.

SEX TALK

ONE EVENING WHEN WE were messing around, I decided to have sex with Bobby. My thoughts were that we're Twin Flames. We will be together forever. Why not have sex? The experience was different than anyone I had ever been with. There was an extreme level of comfort as if I had the memories come back that we had been having sex throughout many lifetimes for hundreds or even thousands of years.

The next day Bobby called me. As usual, I didn't get what I expected. "Are you still having sex with that guy," he asked abruptly. "You need to be wrapping a condom on that guy."

He was talking about Mr. Respectful. "Nice way to start a conversation with me the morning after our first time having sex," I said sarcastically. "To answer your question, no. I'm not still having sex with him. You know that ended a while ago. If you had called and said something about last night instead of bringing up someone from the past, I would tell you how nice it was to finally be with you like that. The night was special to me. Mostly, I was surprised at how comfortable it was to be with you as if we had been having sex for years."

He calmed down with a lower voice. "It was comfortable with you too. But you always make me feel comfortable no matter what we are doing."

I melted.

GASLIGHTING & VERBAL ABUSE

INSTEAD OF COMING CLOSER together, gaslighting started. Usually, he would deny the gaslighted.

One night I caught him by using evidence he couldn't dispute. Bobby mentioned he didn't want my Doberman in his son's room. Chuck left food in his room. My dog would walk in and help himself to a dinner of whatever was left from the night before or the night before that. Chuck's area was disgusting in contrast to the rest of the house which was clean and organized. I was constantly closing his son's door, but it was a losing battle. I was surprised my dog hadn't come down with food poisoning.

Bobby phoned me one day and asked me to buy a dog crate to leave at his house. I bought one the day after he asked and left it in the living area. That night he asked me why I had brought over a dog crate. When I told him he asked me to buy one, he denied it. With his gaslighting over different issues in the past, at times I felt I was going insane wondering if I had forgotten something. This time was different. Bobby records his phone calls.

I put the large metal crate in my car and left that night. I left him a text telling him to listen to his phone recording. I woke up the next morning hearing an apology voicemail. Throughout our relationship, this was one of only two apologies ever. If the call hadn't been recorded, that apology would have never happened, and he would have continued to say he never told me to buy a dog crate.

Besides the gaslighting, flinging verbal abuse in my direction happened regularly. When my desktop computer needed to be replaced, I asked Bobby to take out my hard drive so I could retrieve pictures. I was in my doctorate classes, and his abusive digs would bring me down crushing me under him.

"Why can't you take out the hard drive yourself, Doctor," he asked. "Why don't you know how to do such simple things?"

I stood there looking at him while I felt stupid fulfilling what he wanted me to feel. He never took my hard drive out for me. Any love language of doing

something for me was dead (Chapman, 2015). Helping was replaced with insults.

It took years after that moment to realize that we all have strengths and weaknesses. Computers were not what I had a knack for or any training in.

Even one day when Bobby criticized one of his friends, and he was giving me a compliment, he wasn't able to actually deliver the compliment without dancing around. He just talked about how the friend wasn't smart, and I was different from the friend.

"He's an idiot. Unlike you."

"How am I different?" I asked because my head would spin when he was angry because I never knew if I was the idiot in his eyes at that moment.

"You know. You have that geeky professor

•

vibe."

"So, you're calling me a geek. It seems your friend, that you're angry about is an idiot and now I'm brought into this for some reason as a geek." I was fighting back that day instead of adhering to the rule that arguments end quicker if I stand there and take it like a good slave.

"Geeks are, you know, not idiots."

"Are you saying I'm smart?" I asked in one of many strange conversations with Bobby.

. "Yeah," he said with a shrug of his shoulders showing it wasn't a big deal. Then he quickly changed the subject back to his friend.

When we first dated, compliments flowed often and easily from him while he was love bombing. The love language of affirmations no longer existed (Chapman, 2015).

DATING, DINNERS, & BIRTHDAYS

AT THIS POINT WE had been back to dating each other for a couple of years yet he consistently said he didn't want to date anyone, and he would say he didn't want a girlfriend. Any man from my past wanted to call me his girlfriend. Those relationships moved easily into what seemed normal.

I caught Bobby three times on dating sites right in front of me. He told me that he wasn't getting off dating sites and that I could leave anytime. This was not normal. I was so depressed. I stayed despite my life getting worse. I quit working on my doctorate...a dream since I was first in college before I had my daughter. I spent less time with my daughter and less time with friends. I was up and down depending on how my Twin Flame relationship was going while all along buying into the belief that we were meant to be in what the Twin Flame community calls: Divine Union.

Bobby became cheap sometimes not even paying for a movie ticket complicating things when we wanted to reserve seats online together.

I had to catch him before he paid for one seat. "Reserve two seats. I'll pay for the popcorn and drinks."

"If you want to do things with me," he barked at me one day, "you need to pay for those things."

Were there any men who believed in providing? Support of listening when I had a hard day? Maybe picking up the bill at least half the time?

Many times, Bobby passed me the dinner bill and said, "Pay for dinner." It would get to the point where I was paying for more than half of our meals out even though he had more money, ordered more food, and ordered two or three alcoholic drinks when I rarely drank. In looking at basic math there, it doesn't add up. Boddy didn't align with the man John Gray would describe as doing things for a woman (1994).

Regarding the arguments, twice he argued with me right before my birthday. His birthday is a month before mine. So, we would have his celebration and his gifts. Then my birthday would be skipped entirely with what seemed like a strategy to break up with me one or two weeks before my day. Gifts, another love language, stopped flowing (Chapman, 2015).

On the third year when he tried this, I played a trick on him. I traveled over the summer and had been out of town for his birthday. I purposely didn't care to change plans I had out of town to be with him on his day due to his breakup behavior right before my last two birthdays. I was back in town the a week after his birthday, and of course, I thought all of this through.

It was the Saturday before Father's Day. Having left him in a good mood at his house, I went out with a friend for lunch. When I returned, he made his demands like a whining child when I walked in with a bag. "I hope you have a birthday present in that bag."

"I have a Father's Day card and gift card," I replied with a calm and light demeanor as I ignored his whining. "I figured since our birthdays are so close together, and I was out of town for yours, we could celebrate our birthdays together in a week."

"You can give it to me in the car. I'm hungry. I've been waiting for you to go to a new restaurant."

I didn't know what happened to change his mood during the time I was gone. Since I met a friend for lunch and a walk through the mall, his jealousy was probably part of his problem.

We got in my car when he usually drove. Bobby's car was blocked by Chuck's car. Bobby didn't want to bother the King to move his car.

Once in my car, I handed him his card knowing that smiling and staying in my energy was best. He opened the card, read it aloud with a sarcastic tone, and then did air kisses.

"I guess you're telling me where we are eating with this gift card," he said with the usual darkness in his eyes.

"You can use it anytime with Chuck, me, or whenever. It's for you for Father's Day." I regretted spending $100 on a gift card since this animal was biting at me.

"I want to eat at this new place tonight," he snapped while still sounding like a child crying to mom for a toy.

"That's good with me," I said still trying to stay light and easy. "Just tell me where to go."

I drove to the restaurant. The place was empty except for one other table of people, which made sense because the food was subpar. The manager came over to ask about the meal and have friendly small talk.

"It's been so hot," the manager said as he continued about the little things, "getting older, we are
bothered more by the heat." He talked about age as he looked at Bobby.

I made a joke of it saying, "I'm too young to get what you older men go through being bothered by the heat."

When the manager left, Bobby was angry that I joked about his age. Obviously, I was kidding since I'm the same age. It seemed fine with Bobby when the manager mentioned age.

We ate without talking much. I went to the bathroom and took my time standing in the hallway out of his sight just responding to a couple of texts. I relaxed in the break of being away from him.

•

When we got into my car his rage grew with him becoming more upset about the age joke. I wasn't holding anything back as I told him how ridiculous he was acting. We argued the entire drive home. I would not have engaged in any argument if he were driving because it could have caused him to go off on another road rage incident.

When we arrived back at his house, he told me to leave. We had probably broken up ten times by then. We usually were apart a few days up to a month. We had one break-up of six months and one that lasted two years. The Twin Flames call that the "runner/chaser" stage. One of us would break things off. The other person would chase.

This was year three of no birthday celebration for me. One breakup right before someone's birthday could happen, but three in a row is planned.

HIT YOU IN THE FACE

BOBBY NORMALLY SAT IN his recliner with me sitting on the sofa. After years of being together as friends and discontent partners, the affection, sex, and most communication were over. We would watch television and pet our dogs. Any deep conversation I had was with friends. When I talked about spiritual subjects I was passionate about, he would stare off into space and not say anything. I felt I could be dating a "backdrop person," as

Dolores Cannon discusses (2015).

One night he was in his typical spot, his recliner, with me at a distance on the sofa. As if he was possessed, because it was so random with no argument going on, he said, "Sometimes I want to hit you in the face."

I sat there frozen. Nothing happened. I have no idea what happened after that. He didn't hit me, but why don't I remember what was said after the threat? Time was lost.

After that, I stayed with him even though I wasn't the type of woman to stay with someone like Bobby. The only other man who had tried that kind of thing with me pushed me. I hit him…hard…he was on the floor. That was my normal personality. The hold Bobby had over my entire life was out of this world, and there was nothing Divine about it.

A couple of months later, again with him sitting in his recliner and me on the sofa, he repeated the same statement: "Sometimes I want to hit you in the face." And again, I don't remember what happened after. If there was some blackout, I assume he didn't hit me because there were no marks anywhere on my body after I woke from some zombie state.

Soon after his threats of hitting me, I made plans to move to Sedona, Arizona. Truly waking to the truth, I realized I was in an abusive relationship.

Only days before moving, Bobby started one of his random arguments. "I don't even know why you're mad," I said.

He continued to ramble something as he stood there looking like the lizard that he is. His son walked in and started to interrupt us when I continued not allowing an interruption. "You have to be mad at someone or about something in the world, don't you? If you're not mad at me, you're mad at Chuck, or you're mad the world has done you wrong."

"Don't talk about my son," he snapped.

His son left not wanting to be a part of whatever this was. I laughed. "That's what you got out of what I said." I stood to leave. "I'm leaving before you kick me out."

"No. I'm not kicking you out," he said with his quiet, human voice.

"I'll see you later," I said laughing more and feeling good at not allowing him to bury me down in his Hell anymore. At that moment, I gained a chunk of my power back. But it took two years with complete ghosting of the beast...no contact...to completely dig myself out of Hell and remember who I am.

•

NARCISSIST

I HAVE GATHERED RESEARCH for my studies in college from when in my twenties working on a bachelor's degree, to researching for two master's degrees, and now completing my research for my final doctorate project.

Therefore, why not research Twin Flames from an Earthy perspective utilizing peer-reviewed current research? Whether there is spiritual or alien interference, the following explores only from a research viewpoint to show a grounded, psychological side to the Twin Flame relationship as it relates to narcissism.

Selfish, Rage, and Abuse

Perhaps Bobby was just selfish. However, being selfish is one of the many traits of a narcissist (Carlson, 2022). Even when at the beach, and I was having extreme pain in my eye, the day was still all about him with his comment about me just trying to ruin the day. His birthdays were also important to the point of him being childlike whereas mine were completely skipped for three years.

Besides being selfish, rage is also a potential trait of the narcissist (Stolz, et al., 2021). Bobby raged on towards me usually seeming to have an imaginary story in his mind of problems between us when I felt everything was fine. We were living in split worlds with my world half-full and his not half-empty, but entirely empty. Aggression is higher for narcissists when they are provoked (Kjaervik, 2021). Bobby felt I caused him to get angry before he beat a random man on the road. He blamed me for being responsible for his emotions flying off after I only asked him a simple question about him and his son's mother. He put our lives at risk when driving and when beating a man during road rage.

•

Even when unprovoked, narcissists can be found to be aggressive with abuse not being identified as often as it should be (Kjaervik, 2021). Just as when I was quietly sitting on the sofa, twice he threatened physical violence towards me. In my world, everything seemed fine between us. In his world, his beast was awake as I clearly remember each word that came from his mouth: "Sometimes I want to hit you in the face." Abuse from a narcissistic partner is not identified as often as it should be (Howard, et al., 2022). Research is increasing to support the connection of narcissistic personality disorder to violence towards the partners of the narcissist (Littlebear, et al., 2023).

Narcissism is more common in men than women, which may reflect the reason twenty-seven women were chosen for a qualitative study regarding how their narcissistic partner treats them. Overall, the women expressed experiencing physical, verbal, and psychological abuse. The women described the narcissistic men as controlling, cold-hearted, aggressive, manipulative, deceptive, and "vampires" (Shousha, 2023). My Twin Flame sucking my energy and crushing my soul, comes to mind when seeing the word "vampire." The women in the study needed long-term support to fully recover at the end of relating with narcissistic men. The women also were found to question their reality regarding experiencing gaslighting (Shousha, 2023).

Gaslighting

A person employing gaslighting is more likely a narcissist than not (Shousha, 2023). Gaslighting has been defined as manipulative behavior resulting in confusion and self-doubt (March, et al., 2023). Gaslighting has been associated with abuse within intimate relationships with more men than women viewing the use of gaslighting as acceptable. The victim can become unstable due to the tactics of manipulation and contradiction by the narcissistic partner (Dimitrova, 2021). The story I shared in this book regarding purchasing a dog crate and gaslighting was one of many times I wondered whether I was forgetting or going crazy.

Grandiose

Narcissists look at people, money, and the world uniquely. A common narcissist trait is being grandiose (Anello, 2019). Besides their feeling of grandiosity, a narcissist will chase a situation that gives them status or admiration (Grapsas, 2019).

Bobby had an attitude that the world owed him. In the interview my friend set up with her husband, Bobby acted like he was too good for the job when the job sounded like it was exactly what Bobby had done for a living. He even acted like an expert rider of horses although he never spoke of having ever ridden a horse in our many conversations. Overall, he criticized people, with him always being the better person, and he spent money like it would never run out.

Bobby chose money over time with his son and with me. After adding up the time he was overseas, which started at only six months, his total time out of the country was 3 ½ years. Putting me aside, he was away from his son for an extended time, whereas I couldn't fathom being away from my daughter at that young age for more than a day.

All for money. Money to impress others. Money to pay cash for a house, which he did not do. He came home after working overseas and bought the best of everything: a limited-edition SUV, fast computers, quality large televisions, leather brand-named furniture, high-quality clothing, cigars, guns, vacations…the list goes on. Buying your child the best of everything does not make up for lost time. It is grandiose. I've heard that people on their deathbed don't applaud themselves for accumulating money.

Depressed

Bobby was searching for financial security and a grandiose lifestyle with his lack of self-confidence, in my opinion. He spoke of depression and self-doubt. Depression is common with narcissistic personality disorder (Fjermestad-Noll, et al., 2020). He said he went to bed depressed and woke depressed every day of his life and that he just wanted to stay home in bed sleeping.

Overall, narcissists seem to be living in a world where they process differently than non-narcissists. For me, I was in the cage taking Bobby's abuse and surrounded by his low energy.

One evening, when he was acting depressed and taking things out on me within his nonsensical rambling, the low energy was so heavy I couldn't think. That night the Houston Astros were having their final game of the 2017 World Series. Friends had asked me to meet at a bar and grill we frequented.

I decided to leave Bobby's energy that covered him, covered every square foot of his house, and covered me. I began feeling released from his darkness when I drove only a short distance from his home. The rest of my night was light, easy, and peaceful with friends...and the Astros won the World Series.

TWIN FLAME ALIEN INTERFERENCE: THE LAST MAGICAL MOMENT

WHEN I WAS WRAPPED up in the Twin Flame community, I wanted to see my plan with my Twin Flame to come down on Earth. That vision is listed at the beginning of this book with the title: "Magical Moments of the Twin Flame Journey: Twin Flame Plan to Come to Earth." I now think that vision was a false overlay placed by negative alien beings who trick us into thinking we came here for union into a Divine relationship with our Twin Flame. In my own Twin Flame story in this book, I explain verbal abuse, threats of physical abuse, gaslighting, and ghosting, just to name a few, that I endured for more than ten years.

We could find those traits in people with various psychological issues such as narcissism. Then the spiritual component comes in such as the synchronicities, running into each other, their energy around us, and/or seeing visions. Couple all of that with an online community of people who encourage Twin Flame relationships, and you've concocted a spell of an abusive relationship that we practically beg to stay in. It is way past time to leave the false constraints of the collective community that promotes Twin Flames, and it is time to step out of the cage that aliens created.

The following is a true depiction where I channel what many Twin Flames are going through at this time on Earth. My friend, a healer, Lorice McCloud, assisted me as a guide during the following session. This is what I heard and saw during the session as she questioned me:

Lorice: What are you seeing or hearing regarding Twin Flames?

Angie: It feels like a pit. The words slavery and control are coming to me. I can see Bobby pulling me there. I can hear the word captured. He's taken me out of a higher place. I'm getting that I've been pushed down, held back, manipulated.

Bobby is reptilian. That's the word I hear, and I see that he looks reptilian. It's dark where they are. There are scales on his body. He's powerful in a negative way. He disguised himself to look differently from something he is not so that he looks human. He's full of lies.

They dirty my energy and push me down to be born into a family where I will be held back. There's black all around me as they are pushing me into the lifetime here on Earth. They connect me to false information. I'm supposed to feel like I'm waking and moving forward as I grow to adulthood, but they actually put in a block with this Twin Flame relationship that has sent me off my path. I'm seeing and feeling it is false teaching from the reptilians and the Twin Flame community with them saying the traumas will wake you. But I see this different path where there was a split in time when I met Bobby, and he caused my life to go off

•

my real path.

I see many people are taught the false Twin Flame teachings pulling them off their paths. I see other events pulling people off their paths such as negative political arenas, dysfunctional families, and mundane existences.

Lorie: Is this the only lifetime you've been with Bobby?

Angie: There are other lifetimes where he threw me off my path. There are also imprints or fake memories I see as false where we had a good lifetime together. Those are there so that I think we can achieve happiness again, but that's all false. None of the positive lifetimes actually happened with him.

Lorie: Could he have been taken over before they tried to control you?

Angie: I'm getting that he has more of a reptilian energy. I'm seeing the scales again, a lizard look. It's dark where he lives. He's looking down, and he looks unhappy. Bobby is disconnected from emotion and real attachment. As he looks up at me, he has their eyes instead of human eyes—he has the lizard eyes. There's no compassion in his eyes. He's sitting there before I came into this life...longing for me to be his food.

For the Twin Flames, there was a plan for humans before they came to Earth to have the Twin Flame programming to open at a certain time such as when they become a part of the community. This programming is for the general spiritual audience who is open to allowing Twin Flame negative programming into their lives. The negative extra-terrestrials are doing what they can to hold us back and hold the planet back. I'm seeing the Twin Flame alien takeover as just more false programming thrown out into the spiritual community. People hear about Twin Flames and then connect it with the false programming thinking: I want Divine love. They open themselves up to programming and then get sucked in.

Lorie: I've heard it's seldom that Twin Flames incarnate together:

Angie: I'm looking up there in the spiritual realm. I see a part, an energy of Twins with one in a higher guidance or high self, or mentor assistance level. I am getting the Twin is to be in a positive relation to you instead of a conflict. On Earth, the

Twins are in conflict, which is not the true nature of the Twin Flames. And I'm getting that the label doesn't matter. That is more ego in nature. We all have the ability to have a positive love relationship, but the Twin Flame relationship is taught in the Twin Flame community to start as being full of strife, and difficulties between you, there's a mirroring, the runner/chaser--that is all false teachings.

The right teaching is that a good relationship will start as a good relationship, and it will continue and grow and stay positive with some potential normal difficulties along the way. A bad relationship, as with Twin Flames, will not go from bad to a good relationship. The Twin Flame relationship that the Twin Flame community is teaching, that is created by aliens, can be soul-crushing. It is ruining your life. It can kill you.

Another false Twin Flame teaching is the True and False Twin Flame. That is just another false teaching to keep you sucked in. They will just go from one person to another continuing on the abuse cycle. This is very important to remember so that people do not trade in one bad relationship for another.

Lorice: Is the Twin experience for Earthly

life?

Angie: To expand more on what was shared, I see that once you are out of this body and in a higher place, you are collecting your soul fragments. You are collecting more of yourself. That would be like a Twin, bringing back your pieces. On Earth what I see for some spiritual people is that once you realize you can be alone on Earth, when you are moving towards enlightenment alone on Earth, it's like you're able to shake everyone off, not needing other people, not needing to follow other people, being alone assists you to move to a higher place. As I said, not everyone has to be alone. Many spiritual people on Earth are shedding people, shedding of self, shedding things, and shedding gurus that keep them in the same spot or keep them aligned with false information.

When reaching for another person when you have a lot of work to do on yourself, I don't see it as the way to move forward. And I'm not saying that means people have to always be alone. It's a movement forward. When the movement is obstructed by another person, then there has to be a letting go or the other person has to step up the stairs with you.

Many Twins on Earth will bring up

.

abandonment issues as they come and go. They cheat. They cause many difficulties. The Twin Flame community teaches this is the way it is supposed to be so that growth and movement forward can occur when it actually causes the opposite effect.

It doesn't logically make sense to go into a relationship with someone who is unavailable, with someone who is married, with someone who is abusive, with someone who is unstable. These things don't follow logic whereas the Twin Flame community teaches to put up with all kinds of abuse. The Twin Flame community says it's bringing out what you need to heal when really the community is putting you in a situation to endure a slow death. The negative extra-terrestrials created the Twin Flame community and other negative communities on Earth for their own benefit. They need lower energy to survive.

The aliens have a setup that supports what many humans understand because most people in these Twin Flame communities come from broken homes and broken relationships so these spiritual relationships offer what they had in the past.

Lorice: It's all familiar with a new coat of paint.

Angie: Then there's support from the Twin Flame community that this is how it should be. It's manipulation. I am seeing it being carefully planned by aliens. I'm looking at the alien side beyond just Bobby and the dark entities within the Twin Flame community that support the plan.

To go back to when I was captured, there's a mind wiping of where I came from. It reminded me of a book by Renard where Jesus and Budda were evolving through physical lifetimes growing to enlightenment as they incarnated (Renard, 2017). I see myself in and out of my body accumulating knowledge similar to Jesus and Buddha. Then I'm captured and thrown into a tomb. I was taken when still in a physical lifetime. I was beaten, put in handcuffs, and tortured. My consciousness was pulled out of that body and brought down to a lower reptilian realm. I see a mind wiping as in the Secret Space Programs where they bury my past knowledge through mind wiping and the abuse they did to me. After breaking me, I'm fed the fake Twin Flame vision I saw where Bobby and I made the plan to come here. (Note: I discussed that vision earlier in the book called the Twin Flame Plan to Come to Earth.)

I'm seeing the reincarnation trap of being

•

stuck for a few hundred lifetimes and then coming into this lifetime where I'm starting to gain some of my knowledge and power back. But then Bobby and other aliens came in and infiltrated my path. They aren't all reptilians. There are other types of negative aliens involved as well. There's energy here, not all of it regarding Twin Flames, that is trying to crush souls and hold Earth and the people on Earth from moving forward. The humans are on this slave planet trapped here with many ways to lose their freedom. I see most people trapped here. There seem to be some that are free while most of the Earth is covered in darkness. Those who seem free can cause us to feel we don't deserve what they have. Or we feel something is wrong with us because others aren't trapped. Part of the purpose of seeing those who seem free is to cause us to feel abandoned by the spiritual connection, and this is to cause us to think we cannot create a better life.

A positive energy is on Earth. It was trying to block Bobby from coming into my life here in this lifetime. But I'm hearing from that energy to not get into a savior complex, but on the other side to not lose faith. It's important to keep the faith but also to use your power, keep fighting, and keep moving forward. Help yourself and help others.

Lorice: People will put up with a lot to have a Twin Flame:

Angie: Part of the desire for love is due to an emptiness on Earth, and there is so much hurt on Earth. The human is empty. Thus, humans seek the lower energy love such as what is taught in the false Twin Flame community.

With all the hurt on Earth, love is the opposite. Being alone can be finding the love and balance within yourself. Then humans have the potential to find a higher relationship instead of being in the entity/alien relationship that keeps humans down and feeds off humans. I'm getting confirmation of something regarding people I've met who have been married a long time. Those relationships started good and there was consistency with the relationships remaining good with typical up and downs throughout. But none of those long-term relationships started in a negative way as do the Twin Flame relationships.

There can be love bombing at the beginning of a Twin Flame relationship. But then the relationships go bad. The Twin Flame relationships will not recover and stay in a good place.

•

Lorice: What makes people believe they are with a Twin Flame when their relationship is not good?

Angie: The Twin Flame may love bomb in the beginning and then switch. The Twin who follows, chases, and/or feels more "awake" will trust and feel the love. Then the "Alien Twin," or "Alien Controlled Twin," switches as if you are dating two people. There are two different sides. I see the aliens solidifying the love putting the fake spiritual energy around them that can feel like Divine love, the presence of the Twin with them, the feeling of it being deeper than any other love, and the false energies the aliens place in the spiritual Twin Flame community.

The Twin may love bomb then become negative as the bottom falls out with narcissistic behavior, borderline personality disorder, and/or other traits after the love bombing. This creates confusion.

Regarding humans on Earth in general, not only Twin Flames, I see an alien energy speaking over the soul. It's similar to a black magic energy blanket on people who are coming down here. It's a breathing, live, dark energy keeping people asleep to the truth. The energy is programming humans to:

go to work, come home, struggle, sit and be passive, watch TV, and connect to false beliefs. The air and food are contaminated. People just try to survive. The energy states: If I can't take you down one way (health, families, finances) I will try another (Twin Flames). There are also many gurus online with false teachings or partial truth, yet people will believe all that their guru says.

I see the negative Aliens crushing the souls they collect, recycling, and using souls over and over. The lower energies need the souls as food.

I also see us being in a hybrid program. They considered Bobby and I having a child together on Earth. But instead, three times I became pregnant with him while in this Twin Flame relationship, and the aliens took the embryos. There was a fourth time they tried to take the embryo, but the embryo died. I woke in my bed sick that night confused knowing something had happened to my body. Besides the embryos that were taken during my time with my Twin Flame, many other embryos have been harvested in my lifetime. Humans may feel privileged to have children in a hybrid program. For humans to be taken to a ship and shown hybrid children that were taken from them as embryos, embryos were probably used for other purposes as well such as food.

●

Throughout my life, I went to a ship along with other women. I can see containers going off on what look like conveyor belts. I feel sad seeing this and feel the emptiness of something that is a part of me being taken. There is a sensation of loss as if someone I love died.

Aliens do different things with the embryos. Embryos are checked for quality. A needle is being inserted in some of the embryos to cause them to grow quicker and be released from what seems like artificial wombs. The wombs look organic, but I call them artificial because they aren't women. They might be wombs from Earth animals.

Higher quality babies are auctioned with lower quality babies being sold at a flat rate. Some embryos don't mature into babies, but the organic matter from the embryos is still highly valuable. Those embryos travel through a tube to specific places where they will serve different uses such as adrenochrome for the aliens. Or the embryos can serve a place in the alien medical field. Look at how humans on Earth use cord blood, bone marrow, stem cells, and so forth. A quality human embryo is valuable in ways humans have yet to discover.

Babies are processed to be used for the same reasons as embryos, or babies are raised for purposes such as sex slaves, labor slaves, breeding, or experimentation (as humans do with lab animals).

Many humans think anything that can't be seen or anything from another planet is here to help. They aren't necessarily Angels or positive guides just because you can't see them. Many aliens and beings out there feed off humans in some way. I'm seeing the positive energy of hope coming in again reminding humans to not give up.

Lorice: Seeing the breakdown seems like a huge step:

Angie: It is a huge step once humans see the issues in the world and believe humans can create change. Keep moving forward and letting go of Twin Flames, the Twin Flame community, and gurus. Connect more to your inner knowledge. With gurus only take in what makes sense to your inner self. Connect more to self. We are our own gurus. We touch on certain people or books, gain some info, connect to self, move to someone else, and so on as we grow, learn, and move forward. It's a time of celebration when you leave a guru and move more into your inner knowledge.

Continuous movement is how humans move into higher relationships which is not what is taught in the Twin Flame community.

HEALING & FREEDOM

SUBTRACTING MY TIME IN separations, I spent over ten years tied up in my Twin Flame relationship. A couple of times I've heard he was a False Twin or just some karmic person. Every other time, over ten times, I've had people say he's my Twin Flame. Someone saying we are with a false Twin Flame and now is the time to find your real Twin Flame, is simply more wrong information to keep people in this endless loop. I feel that you must decide for yourself who this person is in your life. Take your power back and leave the collective false reality. Love starts in a positive way. Love doesn't start with love bombing then running and abuse.

At this time, I ghosted the beast two years ago and am free from aliens. I'm certain aliens orchestrated this abusive, controlling relationship, and I feel that the collective Twin Flame community reinforces the negative energy by encouraging people to put up with abusive behavior. I experienced a complete loss of "me" that I've worked to heal after going through hypnosis, energy clearing, and long periods of self-reflection while meditating and journaling.

Most would say it is crazy to consider Aliens planned and controlled Bobby and I. I've been married and have lived with two other men besides my ex-husband. Besides them, I've had many relationships. Throughout all those relationships, I never put up with the kind of treatment I experienced with Bobby. If I never put up with abuse, gaslighting, and so on, from anyone else, why would I then stay with him?

Throughout this relationship, I felt something out of my control holding me there mentally and physically. I was obsessed with being with Bobby, putting him first before me, before my daughter, and before my work. Working through many obstacles while putting myself through college, raising a child alone, and serving in the military, this relationship took over my life chipping away at everything I built for myself.

I hear people online speaking of angels, aliens, and guides as if everything we cannot see or everything that seems spiritual is there to help us. Why do we put so much faith in beings and humans that only show us partial truths or no truth at all? I urge those in relationships with the Twin Flame, to not allow anyone to bring you down into their Hell on Earth.

For anyone reading this, I suggest you do whatever healing makes sense. Take your power back. It is your life. Your soul does not belong to a person or an Alien who abuses, abandons, cheats, gaslights, controls, and ghosts. Everyone deserves love from kind and supportive people who are consistently there for you.

Thank you for reading. I wish you love, joy, and the discovery of your true self. A Twin Flame Journal follows at the end of the print version of this book if you would like to journal your thoughts.

•

ACKNOWLEDGMENTS

George Duisman, an amazing man and the creator of the Consciousness Transformation Technique, gave his healing modality to the world and introduced me to Lorice McCloud in 2018. I am grateful for his generosity and am grateful for this introduction.

I express my deepest gratitude to Lorice McCloud for her assistance in guiding me through the channeled vision near the end of this book.

Through working with clients together, I found Lorice's skills to be immeasurable. Lorice has been the perfect person to show a technique that is similar to hypnosis where she questions me when I am channeling so we can go deeper into the visions and the information. Since Lorice is a psychic, she confirms some of the channeling and assists with expanding the information.

Her assistance with my channeling at the end of this book is aligned with another book we are working on together. That book is our channeling and discussion of the Secret Space and Super Soldier programs.

I would also like to express my gratitude to my mother who had a high level of work ethic and strength I've found to be rare. Even more rare was her willingness to give amazing gifts when she financially had so little. Her positive traits will always be remembered.

Lastly, my father wrote about me in his thesis for his master's degree. I hope to live up to what he wrote. My father's assistance and encouragement with my writing will always be remembered. If I embody the amazing abilities of both of my parents, I will leave this earth with no regrets.

ABOUT THE AUTHOR

Angie Maxfield is a hypnotist who sees clients in person and online. She also spends time writing and loves the outdoors.

Be the first to learn about Angie Maxfield's new releases and receive exclusive content like sneak previews!

www.angiemaxfield.com

References

Anello, K., Lannin, D. G., & Hermann, A. D. (2019). The values of narcissistic grandiosity and vulnerability. *Personality and Individual Differences. 150.* http://doi.org.10.1016/j.paid.2019.06.021

Cannon, D. (2015). *Convoluted Universe: Book 5.* Ozark Mountain Publishing, Inc.

Carlson, R. W., Adkins, C., Clark, M. S. (2022). Psychological selfishness. *Perspectives on Psychological Science, 17*(5). https://doi.org/10.1177/1745691621104569 2

Chapman, G. (2015). *The 5 love languages: The secrets to love that lasts.* Northfield Publishing.

Dimitrova, D. (2021). The women in situations of gaslighting—risk identification in the work environment. *European Journal of Public Health, 31.* 462-463.

Fjermestad-Noll, J., Ronningstam, E., Bach, B. S., Rosenbaum, B., & Simonsen, E. (2020). Perfectionism, shame, and aggression in depressive patients with narcissistic personality disorder. *Journal of Personality Disorders, 34.* https://doi.org/10.1521/pedi.2020.34.supp. 25

Grapsas, S., Brunnelman, E., & Denissen, J. A.

(2019). The why and how of narcissism: A process model of narcissistic status pursuit. *Perspectives on Psychological Science. 15*(1). https://doi.org/10.1177/1745691619873350

Gray, J. (1992). *Men are from Mars, women are from Venus: A practical guide for improving communication and getting what you want in your relationships.* (1st ed.). Thorsons Publishers.

Howard, V., & Adan, Amina. (2022). The end justifies the memes: A feminist relational discourse analysis of the role of macro memes in facilitating supportive discussions for victim-survivors of narcissistic abuse. *Cyberpsychology: Journal of Psychosocial Research on Cyberspace, 16*(4). https://doi.org/10.5817/CP2022-4-10

Kjaervik, S. L., & Bushman, B. J. (2021). The link between narcissism and aggression: A meta-analytic review. *Psychological Bulletin, 147*(5), 477-503. https://doi.org/10.1037/bul0000323

Littlebear, S., Lofties, E., & Mikolon, T. (2024). Counselor perceptions regarding narcissistic personality disorder, narcissistic traits, and domestic violence. *Contemporary Family Therapy: An International Journal, 46*(2), 231-240. https://doi.org10.1007/s10591-023-09667-8

March, E., Kay, C. S, Dinic, B. M., Wagstaff, D., Grabovac, B., Jonason, P. K. (2023). It's all in your head: Personality traits and gaslighting tactics in intimate relationships. Journal of Family Violence, 1, 1-10. https://doi.org/10.1007/s10896-023-00582-y

Renard. G. (2017). *The lifetimes when Jesus and Buddha know each other.* Hay House.

Shousha, N. M. (2023). Now, you can breathe: A qualitative study of the experiences and resilience of Egyptian women victimized by narcissistic relationships. *Journal of International Women's Studies, 25*(1).

Stolz, D. S., Vater, A., Schott, B. H., Roepke, S., Paulus, F. M., & Krach, S. (2021). Reduced frontal cortical tracking of conflict between selfish versus prosocial motives in narcissistic personality disorder. *Perspectives on Psychological Science,17*(5), 1359-1380. https://doi.org/10.1101/2021.03.01.21252656

Van der Weel, F.R., & Van der Meer, A. (2024). Handwriting but not typewriting leads to widespread brain connectivity: A high-density EEG study with implications for the classroom. *Frontiers in Psychology 14.*

•

Twin Flame Hell: Life with a
Reptilian Alien

Made in the USA
Columbia, SC
24 October 2024